W9-BQU-532

GEORGIA Saturdays

Between the Hedges

Foreword by
VINCE DOOLEY

Text by
JEFF DANTZLER

Photos by
RADI NABULSI

www.SportsPublishingLLC.com

Officially Licensed by the
University of Georgia Athletic Association

Publisher:
Peter L. Bannon

Senior Managing Editor:
Susan M. Moyer

Acquisitions editor:
John Humenik

Developmental editor:
Regina D. Sabbia

Photo editor:
Erin Linden-Levy

Book design:
Dustin J. Hubbart

Copy editor:
Cynthia L. McNew

Art director:
K. Jeffrey Higgerson

Cover Design:
Kenneth J. O'Brien

Dust jacket design:
Kerri Baker

Imaging:
Dustin J. Hubbart,
Heidi Norsen, Kerri Baker

Vice president of sales and marketing:
Kevin King

Media and promotions managers:
Jonathan Patterson (regional),
Randy Fouts (national),
Maurey Williamson (print)

ISBN: 1-58261-156-4

The author and photographer would like to express their sincere gratitude to **Chris Hale, Dale Boudreaux, Steve Guyer,** and **James Rohmann** for their invaluable and numerous contributions to this work. *Saturdays Between the Hedges* would not have been possible without the outstanding images created by these skillful photographers.

Printed in the United States of America

Sports Publishing L.L.C.
804 North Neil Street
Champaign, IL 61820

Phone: 1-877-424-2665
Fax: 217-363-2073
Web site: www.SportsPublishingLLC.com

Contents

Foreword

Since Georgia's first football game in 1892, many coaches and players have passed through this great Bulldog program. But the one thing that has remained constant over all these many decades are the Georgia people. The loyalty, spirit, and passion of our people have been captured in dramatic fashion by the photos of longtime Bulldog photographer Radi Nabulsi and the words of Georgia loyalist Jeff Dantzler.

It's the ritual of the fall. They prepare for days and sometimes weeks in advance of each special Saturday. They arise long before dawn in cities and hamlets all across the great state of Georgia as well as neighboring states. They travel both the interstates and the back roads the sometimes hundreds of miles and many hours to the classic city of **Athens.** Like the pioneers in the Old West, they have their special places—

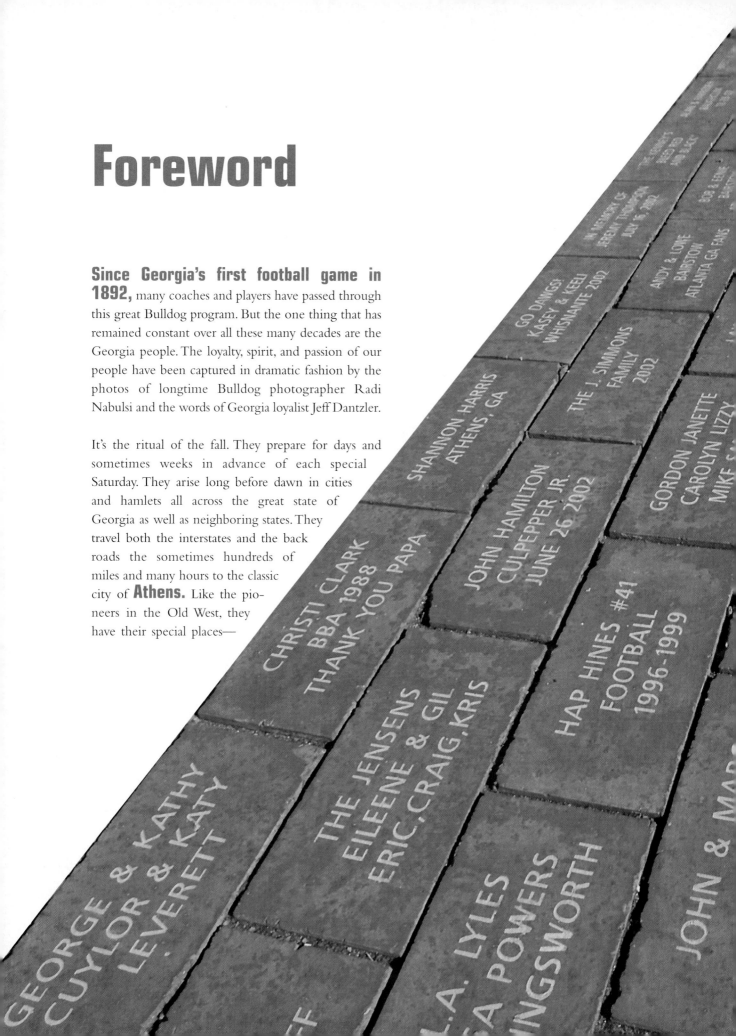

their "claims"—staked out sometimes years and decades ago. Here they meet family, old friends, classmates, and new friends alike. They share the stories of years past, remember good times, and gather around the fold-up table, maybe under a pop-up tent, or perhaps just off the **tailgate of an SUV.** No matter. It's a football Saturday in Athens and it's a special time.

They make their walk to Sanford Stadium—a ritual in itself for many—passing by familiar buildings that hold memories of a time warmly remembered. Casual waves are exchanged with fellow Bulldogs enjoying their own tailgating along the way. They stop by the bookstore or the Tate Center before lining the bridge and 200 yards of pavement to listen to the Redcoat Band and catch a glimpse of the **"Dawg Walk."** Then into the gates of historic Sanford Stadium, where they stop by the Bulldog cemetery, paying tribute to mascots past, gently touch the fabled hedges for good luck, and settle in to watch the Bulldogs, who enter the field through the locker room sign that reads, "Be worthy as you run upon this hallowed sod, for you dare to tread where champions have trod."

Through the pages of this book, you'll feel all the tradition, ritual, and atmosphere of the Georgia football experience—and along with it, you'll get to know and understand the very fiber of the **Georgia people.**

—Vince Dooley
Former Director of
Athletics, UGA

Introduction

From the very first day that it was christened as the home of the Georgia Bulldogs football team, it was clear that Sanford Stadium would be a very special place, a sacred setting for gridiron heroes to be crowned.

Mighty Yale ventured to Dixie as a heavy favorite over Georgia, but **Vernon "Catfish" Smith** scored every point in a 15-0 Bulldog—Georgia Bulldog—victory. Smith went on to be named All-American and fifty years later was inducted into the Collegiate Football Hall of Fame. A legend was born, and Sanford Stadium quickly became a house of magic.

Victories and championships ensued, Saturdays of glory, fueled by players of range from one-hit wonder to All-American and coaches of scale from alumni enraging to **Hall of Fame** qualifying.

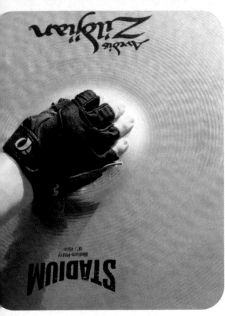

Game day at Sanford Stadium is a special time. But it is much more than touchdowns and turnovers, pylons and penalties, whistles and shoulder pads. Game day at Sanford Stadium is all about pageantry. Tailgating traditions that have been passed on through generations of friends and family. The plush colors of autumn are decorated in Athens with the striking Bulldog colors of **red and black** and the tastes and smells of fried chicken, potato salad, Coca-Cola, bourbon and beer. **The sounds of the redcoat band** marching towards Sanford Stadium, and the echoes of Larry Munson's legendary calls booming from stereos all over the university landscape. Bulldog belles adorn themselves in head-turning attire that would qualify for magazine covers, while leaving no doubt who they're backing. Fall Saturdays in Athens aren't just about the games; it's about the biggest damn party around—about **100,000 strong.** And when the Dawgs win, that's what makes the weekend. The old saying goes, "ain't nothing like being a Bulldog on a Saturday night!"

Happiness and sadness are determined by the performances of these young men. Win or lose, though, everyone comes back next time. It's a chance to **do it all again.** That too is part of the allure.

Game day in Athens means the opportunity to see a whole lot of people that you don't get to see very much. Legendary Alabama coach Paul "Bear" Bryant used to say that no alumni came back to campus to watch some kid take a math test. And nothing brings the Bulldog faithful together like game day at Sanford Stadium. You've always heard that the college years are the **best of your life.** Coming to Athens takes the Georgia faithful back. Best friends, parents, girlfriends (old and new), wives, old college pals and somebody you haven't seen in a long time—all are regulars on game day in Athens.

"I started dating a girl one summer and when it came up that I go to every Georgia football game, she said, 'Well, you won't be doing that this fall,'" Bulldog backer Sonny from Snellville said in 2002. "I broke up with her on the spot."

Georgia would go on to win the SEC Championship and finish **number three nationally** with a sparkling 13-1 record.

Legendary Alabama coach Paul "Bear" Bryant used to say that no alumni came back to campus to watch some kid take a math test.

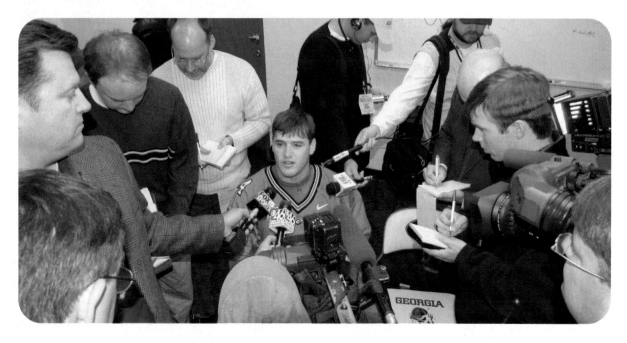

Memories and promise are what stirs such fervor. Great times and magical victories from days gone by and future game days of glory, relishing the championships of **Wallace and Vince** and savoring even more under the watch of Mark **Richt.**

History of Sanford Stadium

From its grand opening on October 12, 1929, Sanford Stadium has been a magical home for the Georgia Bulldog football program. When College Football Hall of Famer Vernon "Catfish" Smith scored all 15 points in the inaugural 15-0 victory over Yale University, it was clear that the Bulldogs would be a formidable force in their home **between the hedges.**

North and South Campus meet in a bowl that forms a natural home for football. With an initial construction cost of $360,000, the grandstands held a robust 30,000 plus great sightlines from the east and west ends and from atop the north and south stands. **The famous hedges** were little more than twigs, sticks and a few leaves at the opening, but they too would grow along with the stadium that would become mammoth.

University trustees had the plan for a stadium intact. The man leading the charge was **Dr. Steadman V. Sanford.** Georgia went 9-1 in 1927, and the Bulldogs were awarded the national championship in the Poling and Board polls. It became clear the Georgia had outgrown its home of **Herty Field.**

Dr. Sanford, who joined the Georgia faculty in 1903, was a great fan of athletics. His career in academia skyrocketed after founding the famed Henry W. Grady School of Journalism in 1921. He served as the University dean from 1927-32. Dr. Sanford was named University president and chancellor, a position he held until 1935, and then served as chancellor for the University System of Georgia. Bulldog historians and UGA brochures and publications referred to Sanford as "the best friend of athletics." He is credited not only with being the most prominent driving force behind the **construction of Sanford Stadium,** but also for bringing mighty Yale "down South" and the school's acclaimed band to Athens for the dedication game between the hedges. It was Yale's first ever trip south of the **Mason-Dixon line.**

It was an easy choice to name the stadium for Dr. Sanford. Certainly a new stadium would not have been built nearly as grand or as quickly without him. As long as Georgia plays football, Dr. Steadman V. Sanford will always be remembered and immortalized as a **"founding father"** of Bulldog gridiron excellence by the grand stadium forever bearing his name.

In the 1940s, Georgia enjoyed one of its greatest decades to this day. Hall of Fame coach Wallace Butts coached the Bulldogs to Southeastern Conference championships in 1942, 1946 and 1948 with college football legends like Heisman Trophy winner Frank Sinkwich, Maxwell Award recipient Charley Trippi, and then-NCAA career passing king Johnny Rauch dazzling the growing Georgia fan base. The Bulldogs won the **national championship** in six polls in 1942 and one in 1946. Trips to the Orange, Rose, Oil, Sugar, Gator and Orange (again) Bowls brought further prestige to the Bulldogs program and established Georgia as one of college football's **top bowl teams.**

Expansion came in 1949, as 6,000 seats were added to the south stands. Unfortunately, the Bulldogs would experience a gridiron **"dark age"**

in the 1950s when losing records—lowlighted by eight consecutive losses to archrival Georgia Tech—dotted the record book. Georgia experienced one last run of glory under Butts's watch by winning the 1959 SEC championship, which was clinched with a last-second Fran Tarkenton-to-Bill Herron touchdown pass to defeat Auburn, a game that still remains one of the most joyous and important in the history of Sanford Stadium.

Georgia hired the **nation's youngest coach,** Vince Dooley, and in his first season in 1964, he led the Bulldogs to a win over Georgia Tech in Athens and the school's first bowl bid in five years. Sanford Stadium would grow to a capacity of **over 43,000.** This would be just the beginning of an expansion boom coinciding with Georgia's growing win total under Dooley's watch.

After the Bulldogs' SEC championship and No. 4 national finish in 1966, Sanford Stadium was double-decked and capacity grew to 59,000. Georgia would win another conference title in 1968. After near misses in 1971 and '75, the Bulldogs again won the league in 1976.

Then came **Herschel Walker** and the magical **national championship of 1980.** Following the unforgettable season, Sanford Stadium was expanded to 82,122. Two more SEC crowns came in 1981 and 1982. Georgia came close for the rest of the 1980s, but did not win another league title. Sanford Stadium's seating capacity remained the same, but the stadium got several aesthetic boosts.

Most notably, for the most highly touted opener in Georgia annals, featuring the 1980 national champion Bulldogs and 1981 national champion Clemson Tigers, **lights were installed.** Georgia won the 1982 classic with the Tigers 13-7 with an injured Herschel Walker playing sparingly with a broken thumb.

Just a few night games would follow, but the lights served yet another big purpose.

"They freed us to play in 3:30 games that served as part of national television doubleheaders," recalls Vince Dooley. "That way **it was no problem** to have the later kickoffs in October and November, and we could finish under the lights when it got dark."

Then came Herschel Walker and the magical national championship of 1980. Following the unforgettable season, Sanford Stadium was expanded to 82,122.

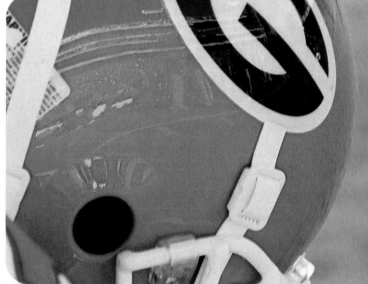

When Georgia entered the 1991 season, the Bulldogs did so with a new seating capacity of 85,434 as the **west end zone was bowled in,** complete with a new scoreboard that has continued to grow into a giant four-poled beacon that serves a dual role, also acting as a massive "nameplate" announcing the arrival on Sanford Bridge to Sanford Stadium and the University of Georgia.

In the 1990s, skyboxes became a must in professional and then collegiate sports. Georgia went first-rate in 1994, constructing double-decked sky suites that tower above the south stands. Expansion to the sky suites would follow in 2000, and Sanford Stadium got a **Sky Club** for donors to enjoy.

Just in time for Mark Richt's second season came a striking east end pavilion addition complete with personalized bricks, granite monument-style walls, and a sterling black iron fence. Georgia would follow with one of its greatest seasons ever, capturing the Southeastern Conference crown and winning a school record 13 games (including a perfect 7-0 slate between the hedges) to **finish ranked number three nationally.** As the Bulldog nation's fervor continued to grow, even more expansion was due. A third deck was added to the north stands prior to the 2003 season, complete with a stylish iron square-spiral staircase that provides popular standing-room viewing. With boxes added between the new deck and second level prior to the 2004 campaign, **Sanford Stadium's capacity grew to over 93,000.**

It's been called college football's greatest spectator stadium. With its sightlines and pitch, and the natural valley encasing the playing field, there is **not a bad seat in Sanford Stadium.** That was the case in 1929, and still is to this day.

With legends like Dan Magill, Dooley and Munson, who have spanned so much of Georgia's history, the past is revered at Georgia. Therefore, the new decks, sparkling sky suites, and high-tech scoreboards and video screens, combine with the sacred hedges, the graveyard for Ugas past, and the view from Sanford Bridge to keep the magnificent stadium both modern and "old school." The past and present continuously meet at Sanford Stadium; that's why it remains a sacred shine to the **Bulldog nation** and one of the grandest facilities in all the land.

Uga and Hairy Dawg

Georgia's most famous face? No question, it's the unparalleled, unrivaled, unmatched mug of the revered and beloved mascot of the Bulldogs, Uga. How strong are the feelings of the Georgia people towards **Uga?** Look no further than the base of the South stands where all of the past mascots are laid to rest in college football's one and only in-stadium cemetery, complete with personalized epitaphs.

Owned by the family of distinguished Georgia alum and prominent Savannah attorney **Frank "Sonny" Seiler,** the Uga line has been the Bulldogs' official mascot since the 1950s. The popularity of the mascot would grow exponentially year by year, and as the Bulldogs' win total grew on the field, so did the attention directed Uga's way.

Perhaps the ultimate shining moment came when Uga V was the cover boy of *Sports Illustrated's* April 28, 1997 issue chronicling the nation's "top jock schools," proclaiming him **America's number-one mascot.** Uga V also became the first collegiate mascot to hit the big screen. Featured prominently in the bestselling book by the same name, Uga made an appearance in Clint Eastwood's *Midnight in the Garden of Good and Evil.* The movie was filmed in Uga's hometown of Savannah and helped his popularity grow all the way to

Hollywood. Uga has long been famous in the bull-dog—as in the actual breed of dog—community. **THE BULLDOGGER,** which is the official publication for the Bulldog Club of America, pro-claimed in 1991 that "the most well-known bulldog in the country is 'Uga,' the University of Georgia mas-cot."

Living and leading a life that many people would be envious of, Uga's game-day attire includes a personal-ized Nike sweater and an **air-conditioned fire hydrant home** at Sanford Stadium next to Georgia's cheerleaders.

Perhaps the ultimate shining moment came when Uga V was the cover boy of Sports Illustrated's April 28, 1997 issue chronicling the nation's "top jock schools," proclaiming him America's number-one mascot.

Game-day weekends begin for Uga on Friday mornings, when he rides with the Seiler family from Savannah to Athens. He stays with the Seilers at The Georgia Center Hotel on south campus, and when it's time to head for the stadium, no Hollywood starlet could possibly turn as many heads as Uga does when heading for the hedges. He poses for **countless pictures** all the way up to the edge of kickoff when it's time to lead the Bulldogs from the locker room onto the field.

A variety of Bulldogs presided over the Georgia football program, including **Butch** (1947-50), **Mike** (1951-55), and whichever fan showed up to the game first with a dog. As recounted by Mr. Seiler, Uga I was given to his wife, Cecelia, by a friend, Frank Heard of Columbus. The first of the pure white English bulldogs would never relinquish his reign that began with the 1956 season opener. University of Georgia immortal historian and legend Dan Magill (who is also the winningest coach in the history of collegiate tennis) recalls a conversation with Hall of Fame coach **Wallace Butts** about Uga becoming the permanent mascot.

"**When I told Coach Butts** he was the grandson of our mascot at the '43 Rose Bowl," he says with a chuckle, "Coach Butts said, 'Well, if his granddad won the Rose Bowl, I want him.'"

Uga I, named **"Hood's Ole Dan"** would preside over Coach Butts's final Southeastern Conference championship team in 1959. He would hand the reins over to Uga II, named "Ole Dan's Uga" during a pregame ceremony in 1966, with the crowd chanting "Damn Good Dog!" Uga II would be at the helm for young coach Vince Dooley's SEC championship powerhouses of 1966 and 1968. Uga III, named **"Seiler's Uga Three,"** became Georgia's mascot in 1973. He would oversee the 1976 SEC championship. His final season would be 1980, the Bulldogs' greatest year. Georgia won the Southeastern Conference title and then beat Notre Dame in the Sugar Bowl 17-10 to capture the national championship. **In his 100th game** of his career, Uga III passed the torch to "Seiler's Uga Four" at the 1981 season opener. Uga III would die two weeks later. Uga IV took the mascot to new heights, making history by becoming the **first mascot to be invited to the Heisman Trophy ceremony** at New York City's Downtown Athletic Club. Georgia's magnificent Herschel Walker received college football's grandest individual award. "The Goal Line Stalker" was flanked by Hall of Fame coach Vince Dooley and a pair of fellow Hall of Fame Heisman finalists in Eric Dickerson and John Elway, but all eyes were on Uga. **Dressed in a full tuxedo,** he stole the show. Uga IV injured a knee ligament when jumping off a hotel bed in 1986 and was sidelined for nearly a month, but Otto "came off the bench" to a 3-1 record as a substitute mascot.

Uga V, "Uga IV's Magillicuddy II," named in honor of the great Magill, took over in 1990. He would go on to be a movie star and grace the cover of ***Sports Illustrated,*** but Uga V's rise to the Bulldog throne was a little hairy. He was the final pup of the last litter sired by Uga IV—and the lone pure white Bulldog. Uga V would turn the reins over to Uga VI, "Uga V's Whatchagot Loran," prior to Georgia's 1999 win over South Carolina. Uga VI at the time of his coronation was far and away **the biggest of all the Ugas,** weighing in at 55 pounds, some 11 pounds heavier than his father with shoulders six inches broader. Uga VI presided over Mark Richt's Bulldogs' SEC championship season 2002, that featured a school record **13 victories.**

Win or lose, there will always be a next game and then a next fall. Uga, like Georgia's continuous quest for championships future and the grand memories of glorious days gone by, is enduring.

The nation's most famous mascot is not Georgia's only mascot. Along with Uga is the giant six and a half foot Hairy Dawg. Debuting in the Bulldogs' national championship Sugar Bowl victory over Notre Dame, **Hairy Dawg** has joined Uga as a staple between the hedges. Though the face of the cheer-leader inside the costume of Hairy is never seen, the right to don it is a major honor.

Hairy Dawg is a constant favorite in national mascot contests and online polls. Donning the face of Uga and a full Georgia football uniform—minus the helmet—Hairy Dawg is a **fan favorite** and nationally famous mascot as well. And when Uga and Hairy Dawg get together, shutterbugs have a field day.

Other Bulldogs are seen throughout Sanford Stadium. At the east end zone, a giant, menacing **granite bulldog**—complete with collar—looms as a constant, well, watchdog between the hedges. Every game when the players and coaches rush from the locker room onto the sacred sod of Sanford Stadium, they run by the massive statue that serves as an ode to the Bulldogs' power.

At the base of the south stands in the southwest corner of Sanford Stadium rests the famous Bulldog cemetery. A **bronze bulldog** statue stands by as a tribute to Georgia's beloved mascots past that will forever maintain a special place between the hedges and in the memories of the **red and black faithful.**

"My favorite memory is the smell of a football game day near the stadium. It's an aromatic blend of fresh-cut grass, fried chicken and whiskey. If you've ever held your dad's hand as you stroll through campus on a sunny autumn day, then you know of what I speak. As the buds begin to bloom, so do visions of Kirby Moore, Paul Gilbert, Andy Johnson, et al."

—"Diamond" Dave Williams, UGA Athletic Association

Traditions

Georgia's athletic department never officially releases any documentation, article, press release or story with Bulldog, Bulldogs, Dog, or Dogs spelled Bulldawg, Bulldawgs, Dawg, or Dawgs. But college football fans across the land have no doubts what **"How 'Bout Them Dawgs?!"** means when seen or heard. The slogan's popularity grew in the Bulldog Nation during the "Wonderdogs'" 9-1-1 thrill-a-minute 1978 campaign and was heard throughout the entire nation as Georgia captured the national championship. Newspapers and magazines from coast to coast proclaimed "How 'Bout Them Dawgs?!" on the heels of Georgia's 17-10 Sugar Bowl victory over Notre Dame. As far as the audible proclamation, just make your way through campus, or into Harry Bissetts, Wild Wing, or The East-West Bistro on **game-day weekends.**

How did Georgia come to be referred to as Bulldogs? To begin with, there were many early ties to Yale University, nicknamed the Bulldogs. Georgia's first president, **Abraham Baldwin,** was a graduate of Yale. And it was no coincidence that Yale christened Sanford Stadium. Historical records credit a couple of Atlanta sportswriters with referring to Georgia as the Bulldogs in 1920, making the nickname stick.

On November 3, 1920, *The Atlanta Journal's* Morgan Blake, while writing about school nicknames, said **"The Georgia 'Bulldogs'** would sound good because there is a certain dignity to a bulldog, as well as ferocity." *Atlanta Constitution* writer Cliff Wheatley, covering Georgia's 0-0 tie at Virginia on November 6, 1920, used the nickname "Bulldogs" in his story five times.

"How 'Bout Them Dawgs?!" can be heard minute after minute on Bulldog Friday nights. And after a big win? "How 'Bout Them Hairy Dawgs?!" heard in beautiful Bulldog harmony with North Campus's famous chapel bell.

This is a tradition that has progressed through **three different centuries.** When the Bulldogs began playing football in 1892, the games took place at old Herty Field on North Campus. The school chapel is located just a few yards away. When Georgia won, freshmen rushed to **ring the chapel bell** until midnight. Even after Sanford Stadium's completion some 37 years later, the tradi-

tion continued. Students, alumni and fans of all ages still hurry to **North Campus** to take part in what just might be Georgia's **oldest tradition.** Now the Chapel Bell rings throughout the night and on into Sunday morning. In fact, on Georgia's giant video board that overlooks Sanford Stadium, a computer-generated image of Hairy Dawg ringing the bell complete with chimes blaring over the public address system announces with authority yet another **Bulldog victory.** But just like in 1892, ringing the Chapel Bell following Bulldog victories is a signature part of Athens game weekends.

When Georgia won, freshmen rushed to ring the chapel bell until midnight. Even after Sanford Stadium's completion some 37 years later, the tradition continued.

The sounds of Georgia include a wide assortment of songs with artists ranging from The Redcoat Band to Bulldog crooner Clisby Clarke to Athens songwriter Mike Dekle all the way to "The King of Soul" himself, James Brown.

"Glory, Glory," sung to "The Battle Hymn of the Republic" is Georgia's official fight song, and records back to the 1890s chronicle its playing and singing at Bulldog games. Other Redcoat Band tunes that permeate throughout Sanford Stadium, like **"Hail to Georgia,"** excite the Bulldog faithful. But many other songs that can be heard blaring through boom boxes and car stereos at various tailgates make the Georgia people smile.

BETWEEN THE HEDGES   **39**

"Feelin' frisky in the Sanford sunshine, havin' a Georgia good time," are words to remember from Clarke's "Bulldawg Boogie."

His most famous hit—"Bulldawg Bite," featuring the chorus of "hunker down hairy dawgs"—is an anthem second only to "Star-Spangled Banner" for the sons and daughters of Georgia.

Athens insurance agent Mike Dekle, who has written such country hits as "Don't Love Make a Diamond Shine," and "Scarlett Fever," penned a catchy tune, "Donnan's Dawgs," which then became "Georgia Dawgs."

Ask Bulldog fans what their favorite James Brown song is and neither "Sex Machine" nor "Living In America" would be the answer. **"Dooley's Junkyard Dawgs,"** written, sung and performed during Georgia's 1976 run to the Southeastern Conference championship still brings back great memories. "The Junkyard Dawgs," coined by legendary defensive coordinator Erk Russell for his over-achieving defenses of 1975 and 1976, is a nickname still synonymous with Georgia football. So when Brown, an Augusta native and big Bulldog fan, wanted to pay tribute, it seemed a natural to pay homage to Dooley's Junkyard Dawgs.

Those Junkyard Dawgs wore white pants, as did every team coached by Dooley starting upon his arrival at Georgia in 1964. But prior to the Bulldogs national championship run in 1980, Dooley reinstituted an old Georgia tradition—"Silver Britches." Hall of Fame coach Wallace Butts clad the Bulldogs in silver pants upon his arrival at Georgia in 1939, and they were a trademark of his four Southeastern Conference championship teams. Dooley, also of course a Hall of Fame coach, won three of his six SEC titles with Herschel Walker, Terry Hoage, Kevin Butler, Buck Belue and crew wearing the silver britches. Mark Richt, who has certainly put together a resume that could land him in the College Football Hall of Fame, led the Bulldogs to the **2002 SEC crown** with the **silver britches.**

The young men who play in the silver britches play in one of the grandest settings in all of college football, Sanford Stadium. With English privet hedges encasing the field, playing **"between the hedges"** is a term coined by the legendary Grantland Rice nationally known as a date with the Bulldogs in Athens.

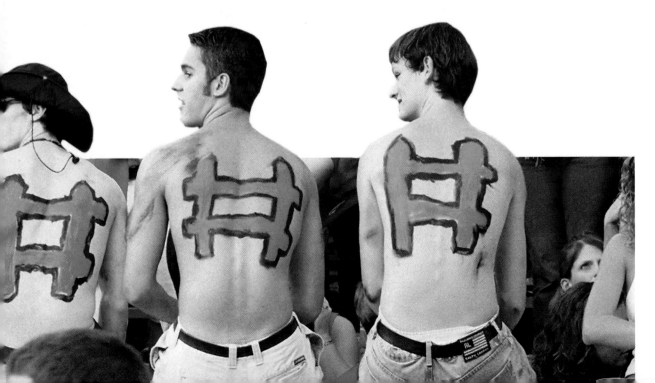

Georgia's grandest legend, the great Dan Magill, in the fashion of Harry S. Truman's "The Buck Stops Here" nameplate, always had showing on his office desk an impeccable quote from the great British Bulldog–the famous Winston Churchill quote, **"The nose of the bulldog is slanted upwards,** so that it can breathe without letting go."

"How 'Bout Them Dawgs?!"

First Friday and the Dawg Walk

Mark Richt was hired as Georgia's head football coach the day after Christmas in 2000. His success at Georgia was instant. The Bulldogs set the table in his first season, going 8-4 with wins at Tennessee and Georgia Tech. The following year, Georgia won a school-record 13 games while capturing its first Southeastern Conference championship in 20 years and finishing ranked No. 3 nationally. On the field was not the only place where Richt had an instant impact. While embracing Georgia's past, he brought a pair of new traditions.

"First Friday" was instituted prior to the 2002 championship campaign. Held annually in conjunction with the UGA Alumni Association, the event takes place in the Stegeman Coliseum the Friday night before Georgia's first home football game. Jon Stinchcomb—All-American, Academic All-American and one of Georgia's captains in 2002—proved prophetic when addressing the throng the night before the Bulldogs' thrilling 31-28 victory over Clemson to open the magical campaign, promising that **"we'll play like champions!"**

Taking place an hour and a half prior to each game at Sanford Stadium, the "Dawg Walk" serves as an amazing adrenaline rush to players and fans alike.

Richt's most popular implementation, though, is undoubtedly the "Dawg Walk." Taking place an hour and a half prior to each game at Sanford Stadium, the **"Dawg Walk"** serves as an amazing adrenaline rush to players and fans alike. Upwards of six to seven thousand fans stuff the Tate Center parking lot beyond **Sanford Bridge** and the West end zone. Much like Charlton Heston eluding Yul Brynner in *The Ten Commandments,* the fans part and a walkway is formed, lined by the Redcoat Marching Band. Georgia's cheerleaders lead the procession with the coaches and team following. A massive outbreak of goosebumps always ensues, and whether or not the **Dawgs** are ready to play is not an issue.

"I don't miss the Dawg Walk," says long-time Georgia fan and fervent tailgater Rob Sherrell of Athens.

Once it became established, the Dawg Walk has indeed become a "can't miss" for many Georgia fans. In the second and third seasons of its establishment in 2002 and 2003, the Bulldogs posted a perfect 13-0 combined record **between the hedges.**

"It's a big part of game day," said Georgia coach Mark Richt. "It really helps get our players fired up and ready to play."

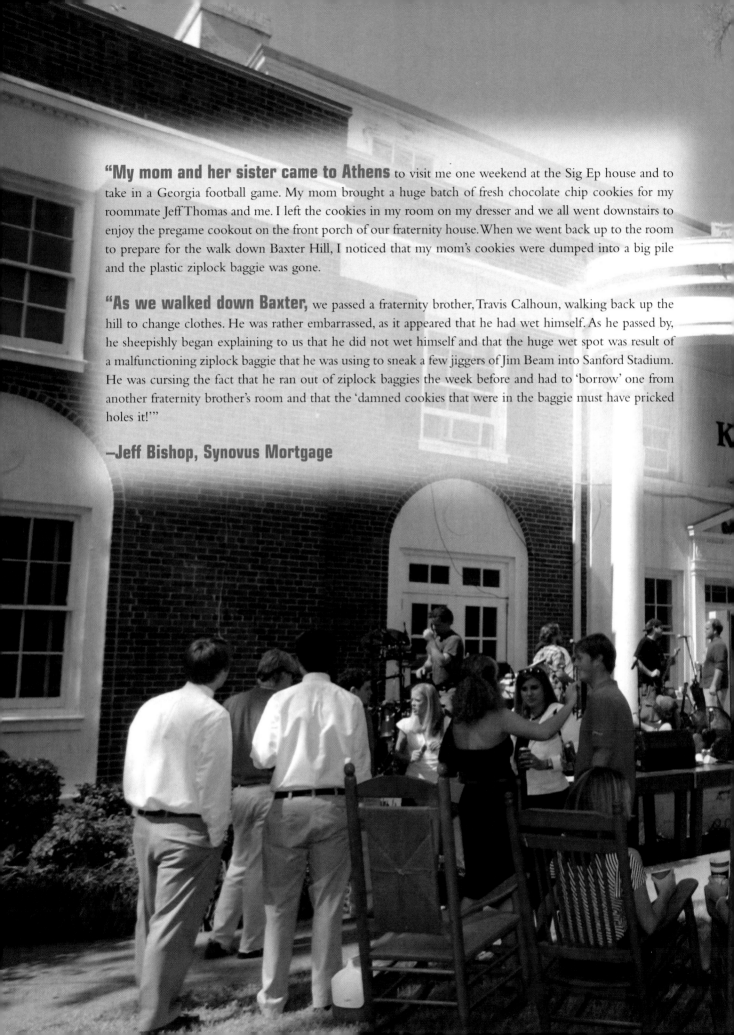

"My mom and her sister came to Athens to visit me one weekend at the Sig Ep house and to take in a Georgia football game. My mom brought a huge batch of fresh chocolate chip cookies for my roommate Jeff Thomas and me. I left the cookies in my room on my dresser and we all went downstairs to enjoy the pregame cookout on the front porch of our fraternity house. When we went back up to the room to prepare for the walk down Baxter Hill, I noticed that my mom's cookies were dumped into a big pile and the plastic ziplock baggie was gone.

"As we walked down Baxter, we passed a fraternity brother, Travis Calhoun, walking back up the hill to change clothes. He was rather embarrassed, as it appeared that he had wet himself. As he passed by, he sheepishly began explaining to us that he did not wet himself and that the huge wet spot was result of a malfunctioning ziplock baggie that he was using to sneak a few jiggers of Jim Beam into Sanford Stadium. He was cursing the fact that he ran out of ziplock baggies the week before and had to 'borrow' one from another fraternity brother's room and that the 'damned cookies that were in the baggie must have pricked holes it!'"

—Jeff Bishop, Synovus Mortgage

Game Days

There is something wonderful about the smell of **fresh-cut grass** on an Autumn Saturday morning. At Sanford Stadium it signals the start of another game between the hedges. The past meets the present on those special half-dozen autumn saturdays. Fellowship abounds, as friends have an entire weekend to share their common passion. For those fans out early, trekking across **Sanford Bridge** is a special treat. The aroma permeating from the sacred sod richly mixes with the sights of the stadium.

Fans of all ages, shapes and sizes flock to Sanford Stadium. Friends of today and years gone by meet for those special autumn Saturdays. Game days represent a wonderful opportunity for parents and their children to come together. It's a time and place for grown men to **paint their faces** and wear hats that any other day of the week might be considered somewhat funny. Little boys wear their jerseys and inflatable helmets and little girls don cheerleader outfits. One day they just might be performing **between the hedges.** They will always remember this day—this game day.

Little boys wear their jerseys and inflatable helmets and little girls don cheerleader outfits. One day they just might be performing between the hedges. They will always remember this day—this game day.

Memories come flying back. As a youngster, seeing Herschel Walker, Terry Hoage, Kevin Butler, Lindsay Scott and Buck Belue perform their magic between the hedges created memories that will last a lifetime. Season by season, game by game, the memories grow. A David Pollack big play on defense in 2003 stirred memories of one made in the same spot between the hedges by Terry Hoage in 1983. A dazzling touchdown run by **The Goal Line Stalker** Herschel Walker, against Georgia Tech in 1982 culminated in the same west end zone under a similar sky as a David Greene to Fred Gibson touchdown connection against the Yellow Jackets in 2002.

As memories like these mount, you return to those youthful days, hearing older fans talking about the exploits of Trippi, Sinkwich, Tarkenton, Stanfill, Scott, Cavan, Greer and Andy Johnson. The championships those players won and how they did it, and how that compared to the exploits of Walker and Hoage. You remember thinking, that seems so long ago. It's easy to imagine Herschel and Hoage and Belue and Butler seeming a long time ago to today's **youthful Bulldog fans.**

As time goes on, the memories are more than just the game. You flash back to going to games with your dad and then friends from home. Then came those wonderful **college years** when lifelong friends were made. More and more of those Saturdays become weekends. Friends and tailgates and those great Friday night dinners add up over the years. Game weekends, as time goes by, become much more than just the game.

Friday afternoons, the cars, SUVs, and campers come rolling into Athens with the car flags whipping in the wind. The cocktails start flowing early. Not many people work until 5:00. Highway 316—"The Hunker Down Highway"—stretching from Atlanta to Athens is jam-packed at every light. The drive from South Georgia through towns like Ludowici, Wrens, Statesboro, Thomson, Monticello and Crawford seems so lengthy, with Athens awaiting like a **city of gold.** In the old days, the first part of the classic city you could see rolling over a hill on the east end of Clarke County was the **old green C&S sign.** It's long gone now. But for many years it was the first signal that arrival to heaven on Earth was at hand.

Tailgating

A rush to the senses comes with the onset of **autumn** in Athens. The sounds, smells, tastes, feelings, and, oh yes, the sights of game days at the University of Georgia are very special to the sons and daughters of the **red and black.**

Start with the electricity that shoots through campus and downtown Athens thoughout the week of a game. "Georgia weekend Friday night, Dawg people start feelin' right" (as Clisby Clarke so aptly described in his classic ode to Georgia Football, "Bulldawg Boogie"), categorizes the mood perfectly. Vibrant and energized, old friends converge with the edge of kickoff anticipation thickening the air. Campers and recreational vehicles come rolling in, and there are more flags flying from car windows than there are at New York's United Nations Building. The cocktails and stories flow. Who knows who you'll see? For the Georgia people, there is nowhere on Earth they would rather be.

The cobwebs shake out easy on the day the Bulldogs play. Time to start again. **Fried chicken,** barbecue, beer, bourbon, pimento cheese and potato salad smell wonderful and taste great. The brilliant colors of fall blend beautifully with the **red and black** that shine on the striking landscape of the Georgia campus, rich in undulating hills and majestic pines, oaks and magnolias.

Heads turn and—just for a moment—football moves off the mind, as the beautiful women of Georgia stroll from tailgate to tailgate stylishly clad in red and black ensembles straight out of an *InStyle* sports section. What are you going to wear? That's the question for Bulldog Belles as they dress to shine—in **red and black** of course.

Redcoat Band drums rhythmically rattle while the immortal calls of the legendary voice of the Georgia Bulldogs, Larry Munson, bounce from stereo to stereo. Within two syllables, any Bulldog over the age of 12 can tell you the game, play and score.

As game time approaches, Sanford Stadium fills, swells and then overflows with **93,000-plus** in emotional orbit. Just minutes before kickoff, a lone **Redcoat trumpet** player stands in the northwest corner of Sanford Stadium and performs "The Battle Hymn of the Bulldog Nation." The soloist leads into a rousing presentation on Sanford Stadium's massive video board, showcasing Georgia's gridiron moments and narrated by none other than the mighty Munson, inciting a massive, widespread outbreak of goose bumps.

Somehow the smells of plastic bag-encased bourbon, cigarette smoke and peanut hulls produce a **wonderful aroma.**

As game time approaches, Sanford Stadium fills, swells and then overflows with 93,000-plus in emotional orbit.

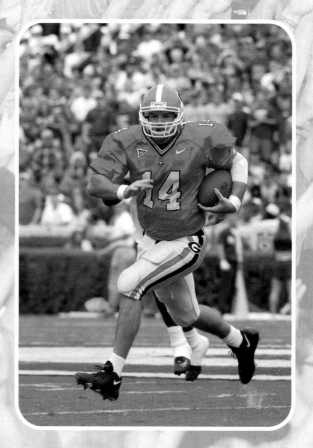

For the next few hours, it's up to the players. If the Dogs win, all is well. It's amazing how much happiness and sadness revolves around the performance of young men in their teens and twenties. When the news is good, the good times keep on rolling.

Serenaded by the **chapel bell's chimes,** the tailgates and parties roll on through the night, well into Sunday morning. Some cold fried chicken and one or two more? You bet.

And you can't wait until next time.

"**I played youth football** at the Athens YMCA and I was lucky enough to be able to wear Herschel Walker's number (34). We played on game day prior to the kickoff. I don't remember who Georgia played that day, but what made it more memorable was that I scored a touchdown that day—in Sanford Stadium—in front of a large crowd. It was great and the next best thing to being a Dawg!"

—Joey Conglose, UGA grad and Athens businessman

Pregame

The games before the game often play a large part in the outcome of the contest. Whether or not a team is ready to play is especially easy to see early in the game. Very few pregame speeches are of the fire and brimstone nature of those delivered by Knute Rockne to **"win one for the Gipper."** A calm before the storm, much like the huddle's prelude to the play, with the players kneeling around the coach. When the last word is spoken, it's time to rush the field.

Gathering by the big granite bulldog at the east end of Sanford Stadium, the goosebump factor skyrockets beyond the hedges while the band plays "Krypton." Then comes "Glory, Glory!" and the rush through the sign. Led onto the field by Uga and the Georgia cheerleaders, the players dash through a red and black "tunnel" lined by the Redcoat Band. At this point, the stadium is **absolutely rocking.** An emotional fever pitch is reached and the long wait for kickoff is over.

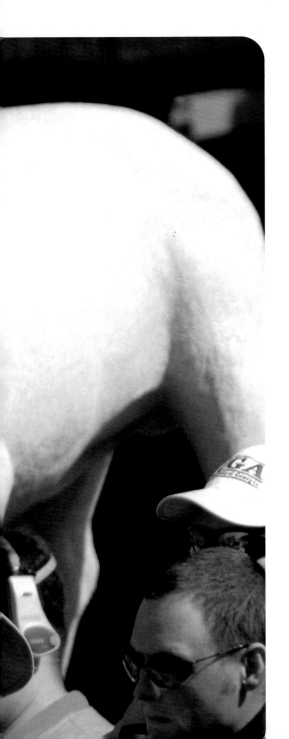

In the stands, before the players emerge, the national anthem puts things into perspective. When the band plays "The Star-Spangled Banner," it's a Sanford Stadium **tradition** for the crowd **to sing along.**

When the uproar comes to a hush once the team has come onto the field, the captains gather at the big "G" at the 50-yard line. Then comes the pregame huddle and prayer. Then comes the kickoff.

Well before, though, the field is crowded even when the stands are not. The players stretch and warm up. Concessioners and **security personel** mill about. In the press box, the television cameras are checked, and the sportswriters arrive, digesting the mountains of information distributed by the Georgia sports information office.

Game time is in sight.

Many more than the **93,000** in attendance will watch or listen to the game. Even more than that will read about it.

Upwards of 100 media members routinely cover Georgia games. A vast majority of the Bulldogs' contests are televised nationally, bringing immeasureable publicity. Dozens of photographers line the playing field, adding the pictures to the words that will be digested by oh so many Georgia fans. And of course there is the massive Georgia Radio Network with over 100 stations. Riding for over four decades on the words of "the legendary voice of the Georgia Bulldogs, **Larry Munson,**" delivered with the booming signal of Atlanta flagship station WSB, the Georgia Bulldog radio network has more stations than any in the country. For the folks who can't make it to the stadium, listening to Larry Munson on the Bulldog radio network has been a Saturday way of life for many, many years. And you always see a lot of head-phones in **Sanford Stadium.** Listening to Munson while watching the game brings the best of both worlds.

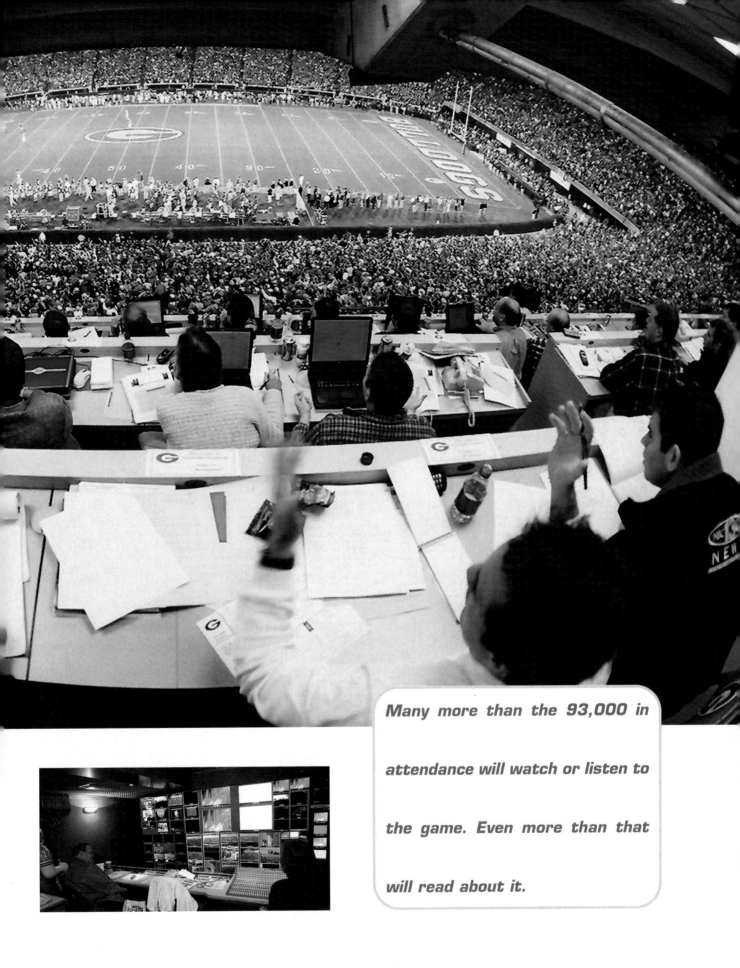

Many more than the 93,000 in attendance will watch or listen to the game. Even more than that will read about it.

Football players aren't the only Bulldogs clad in red and black uniforms on game day. Acclaimed cheerleaders, dance-team members, The Georgettes and the famous Redcoat Band all work extremely hard to put on quality pregame, in-game and half-time performances. The flags with Bulldog heads, the Georgia **"G"** and **"Go Dawgs!"** fly en mass. The field is awash in a sea of red and black. The Redcoats play on, while the cheerleaders do just that, the baton twirlers put on their show, and the dance team performs their long-rehearsed, choreographed routine. **Uga** brings smiles with his customized Georgia "G" red and black Nike sweater. Hairy Dawg is on the move, whether he is dragging a stuffed Tiger, playing with and petting Uga by the giant fire hydrant, or hugging a cheerleader. All of this is a major part the pagentry that helps make college football so special.

Games

Is there anything so splendid as a sun-splashed Sanford Stadium Saturday in which the sons and daughters of Georgia celebrate a Bulldog victory? Encased by the famed hedges in the valley of one of America's most **massive athletic arenas,** the rich green sod serves as the battle ground for modern-day gladiators performing amidst an electric atmosphere of unbridled pageantry.

As the players take the field clad in the red jerseys and red helmets—surrounding the white oval with the legendary **"G" logo**—complemented by the striking silver britches, the sunshine bounces off the attire. The colors are brilliant. The red, black and silver on the green, squaring off with heated ferocity against the crimson and white of Alabama, blue and white of Kentucky, Auburn's burnt orange and blue, the old gold and black—or is it navy blue—of Tech, and garnet and black of South Carolina. **It's brilliant imagery.**

As the players take the field clad in the red jerseys and red helmets—surrounding the white oval with the legendary "G" logo—complemented by the striking silver britches, the sunshine bounces off the attire.

Huddles represent the calm before the storm. The offense and defense line up. Receivers and fullbacks slide into motion. The fullback stops to form an off-set "I." The flanker continues to drag. If the cornerback moves with him, that means the defense is in "man-to-man" coverage. If the corners don't move, it's a zone. A linebacker jumps on to go face to face with the tight end. **Will he blitz?** Will he drop into coverage? Or will it be a run?

Then comes the snap. Then comes the fury. A typical play usually lasts five to 10 seconds. The power, speed and force are **swift and fierce.**

Exhilaration after first down, sack, interception, or the ultimate, a touchdown with the massive throng of **93,000-plus screaming** at the top of their collective lungs, delivers feelings of unbridled elation—both between and beyond the hedges. **Joyous sounds of thunder.**

"O. Henry once wrote, 'You can't appreciate home 'til you've left it, money 'til it's spent, your wife 'til she's joined a woman's club, nor Old Glory 'til you see it hanging on a broomstick on the shanty of a consul in a foreign town.' Being a recent grad of the University of Georgia, those words haunt me. The hardest thing I ever had to do was leave home and go to college. Now, if I had only one wish, it would be to leave my new home and go back to college. I have a feeling many feel the same way I do. God's therapy for this longing is college football. For a couple of weekends during the fall, that wish comes true, and our dreams become real-ities. Is that heaven? No, it's Athens."

—Clay Brindger, UGA Class of '03

Larry Munson

For all of the **great players** like Herschel Walker, Charley Trippi, and David Pollack and the legendary coaches like Vince Dooley, Wallace Butts and Mark Richt, a man who never donned the silver britches, nor stalked the sidelines is as beloved as any Georgia football figure ever. Larry Munson began his career as Georgia's **play-by-play** announcer in **1966,** replacing the popular Ed Thilenius. Over the next several years, his brilliance behind the microphone and growing love for Georgia endeared him to the Bulldog faithful.

The Bulldogs' third consecutive Southeastern Conference championship was clinched on the plains with a heartstopping 19-14 victory over Auburn in 1982 with Munson pleading with Georgia to **"hunker down one more time!"**

Many magical Bulldog moments are remembered as much by the calls of Larry Munson as they are for the plays themselves. There was "Appleby to Washington," when the latter "ran out of his shoes" in delivering a 10-7 upset victory over Florida in 1975. Three years later, the **Bulldog nation** rode on his every word on the closing drive that set up Rex Robinson's game-winning field goal to defeat Kentucky in 1978 with "the whole stadium standing; naw, some of 'em are upside down, but they're tryin' to stand." In 1980, it was the mighty Munson who introduced the sons and daughters of Georgia to **"The Goal Line Stalker,"** "five, 10, 12, he's running over people, oh you Herschel Walker!"

Later, during the Bulldogs' run to the national championship, Buck Belue hit Lindsay Scott for a 93-yard touchdown pass to deliver an unbelievable 26-21 comeback victory over Florida.

The **greatest play** in Georgia history and one of the most famous in collegiate football annals is immortalized by the unforgettable call of "Run Lindsay! Lindsay Scott, Lindsay Scott, Lindsay Scott!" The Bulldogs' third consecutive Southeastern Conference championship was clinched on the plains with a heartstopping 19-14 victory over Auburn in 1982 with Munson pleading with Georgia to "hunker down one more time!"

No arena has featured more headphones than Sanford Stadium, with a mass contingent of the Georgia people tuning in while watching to "get the picture." If the Georgia football program is a body, **Larry Munson will forever be its voice.**

Vince Dooley

Very few football coaches can say they spent 25 years at one school. Very few athletic directors can say they spent **25 years** at one school. Very few men can say they actually spent 10 years doing both. **Vince Dooley** can say all of this.

A member of the Collegiate Football Hall of Fame, Dooley was the unlikely hire at the age of 31. In his first season at the helm in 1964, the Bulldogs beat Georgia Tech and won in their first bowl game in five years. The following season, Dooley's Dawgs used the famous **flea-flicker** play and ensuing two-point conversion to defeat Paul "Bear" Bryant's national champion Alabama Crimson Tide. Georgia would then defeat Michigan in Ann Arbor, rediscovering a place on the national football landscape. The stage was set, and the Bulldogs won the Southeastern Conference championship, going 10-1 and finishing ranked **No. 4** nationally in Dooley's third season. Two years later Georgia would win another SEC title. The Bulldogs came close in 1971 and 1975 before capturing the third conference crown under Dooley's watch in 1976. Georgia would knock on the door two more times, and then Herschel Walker signed with the Bulldogs on Easter Sunday 1980. The Dogs would win the national championship and three straight SEC titles. From 1980-83, Georgia posted a 43-4-1 record, the best in the nation and the greatest era in Bulldog football history. Dooley's teams would go on to **five bowl games** in his final five seasons, and his final resume is one of the best in the history of the SEC: a 201-77-10 record, six Southeastern Conference championships and the 1980 national title. He was named SEC **Coach of the Year** seven times and joins Bryant, Tennessee's General Robert Neyland and Ole Miss's Johnny Vaught as the only league coaches to win conference titles in three different decades.

He was named **SEC Coach of the** Year seven times and joins Bryant, Tennessee's General Robert Neyland and Ole Miss's Johnny Vaught as the only league coaches to win conference titles in three different decades.

As **athletic director,** he oversaw a tremendous growth at Georgia in all aspects during the television and women's sports boom that began in the 1980s. Sanford Stadium underwent a tremendous growth spurt with Dooley in the athletic director's chair. National and Southeastern Conference championships became the norm with a phenomenal group of coaches and athletes carrying the torch for Georgia both between and beyond the hedges. Championships, honors, accolades and top-of-the-line, state-of-the-art facilities will forever mark Dooley's legacy. He's given the Bulldog Nation countless smiles. And at the time of his retirement in June of 2003, Dooley was beaming with the Bulldog Nation at coach Mark Richt and the Georgia football program. In 2002, Georgia won the SEC title, a school-record 13 games and **No. 3** national ranking. The following year, the Bulldogs would finish No. 6 and win 11 games. It marked Georgia's greatest run in back-to-back seasons since the **Bulldogs' magical run** under Dooley from 1980-83.

That's Vince Dooley. He has been a symbol of Georgia's championship past while helping build title-winning programs of the future.